Re-Craft

unique projects that LOOK great

(AND SAVE THE PLANET)

BY JEN JONES
AND
CAROL SIRRINE

CAPSTONE PRESS
a capstone imprint

Re-Craft

unique projects that Look great

(AND SAVE THE PLANET)

BY JEN JONES AND CAROL SIRRINE

Table of Contents

Old Clothes

When it comes to protecting the planet, everyone can help. Every day you can choose to follow the three Rs of caring for the environment: reduce, reuse, and recycle. It's not hard to make the world a better place.

Reusing old items can be fun! Thrifty crafters have found ways to reuse items and keep them out of the trash. With a little creativity and a few craft supplies, you can recycle trash into treasures.

Reusing old T-shirts and jeans reduces waste and helps keep the environment healthy and clean. The projects in this book are only a taste of what you can do with old clothes. You're sure to come up with more ways to reuse your favorite old T-shirts and jeans. And you'll be doing your part to save the environment—one T-shirt and one pair of jeans at a time!

Go Metric!

It's easy to change measurements to metric! Just use this chart.

To change	into	multiply by
inches	centimeters	2.54
inches	millimeters	25.4
feet	meters	.305
yards	meters	.914

T-Shirt Terms

1. Sleeve hem
2. Sleeve seam
3. Collar
4. Shoulder seam
5. Underarm seam
6. Side seam
7. Bottom hem

Jeans Terms

1. Outer side seam
2. Belt loop
3. Waistband
4. Front pocket
5. Inner side seam
6. Back pocket
7. Center back seam
8. Hem

Kickin' Kozies

You don't have to go back to the 1980s for a great pair of leg warmers. No matter the weather, leg warmers are sure to make a style statement. Worn with skirts or jeans, these recycled T-shirt leg warmers will get you noticed.

Here's what you need:
- 1 large T-shirt, at least 18 inches wide
- ruler
- chalk
- fabric scissors
- 2 safety pins
- needle and thread

Step 1

Lay T-shirt flat on a table or cutting surface. Use ruler and chalk to mark a 14-inch by 18-inch rectangle, using the bottom hem as one of the long sides. Cut along chalk lines, making sure to cut through both layers.

Step 2

Separate the fabric so you have two pieces. Fold the pieces in half lengthwise with right sides facing in. Line up the long edges and pin closed. Sew the pinned edges together with small stitches about ½ inch from edge. Remove pins. (See sewing instructions on page 19.)

Step 3

Turn right sides out and lay one leg warmer flat with seam on left side edge. Fold the seamed edge over 1 inch. Make very small cuts every inch on the new fold, not including the hem. Make sure to cut through all layers. Repeat with the second leg warmer.

Step 4

Cut two 1-inch by 36-inch strips from leftover fabric or scraps from other projects. Pull the ends of the strips to stretch and curl. Attach a safety pin to each end of one strip.

Step 5

Lay the seam flat so you can see the holes along either side. Using a strip you cut in step 4, lace up the sides of one leg warmer like an athletic shoe, starting at the hemmed edge. Repeat with other leg warmer.

Step 6 *(not pictured)*

You can adjust the fit of the leg warmers by pulling the laces tighter or making them looser. Pulling the laces tight at the top will help them stay up.

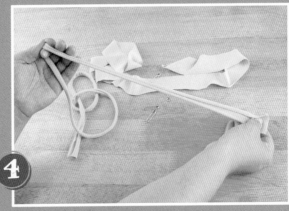

Tip: For cozier leg warmers, try using an old sweatshirt.

Jean Jacket

From your clothes to your shoes to your hair, you like to show off your style. Now you can dress up your school supplies too. Adding a jean "jacket" is a fun and easy way to make a boring binder shine.

Here's what you need:

- fabric scissors
- old pair of jeans
- 3-ring binder
- pen
- ruler
- glue gun and hot glue
- decorations or jean pockets

1

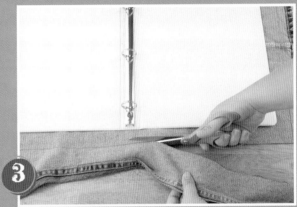

Step 1
Cut off a pant leg. Cut along the outer seam to create a flat piece of jeans material.

Step 2
Place an open 3-ring binder on top of the material. Use a pen to draw an outline of the binder on the jeans. The outline should be about 1 inch wider than the binder.

Step 3
Cut out the material along the pen mark.

Step 4
Hot glue the material to the binder. Hold the binder partially closed as you glue.

Step 5
Decorate the front of the binder using back pockets or decorations cut from old jeans.

T-yarn Scarf

Scarves add style to any fashion trend. For this scarf, start with super-soft yarn made from old T-shirts. T-yarn is great for knitting, crochet, or any other way you use yarn. Use T-yarn to make this chic scarf. It can also be made into a headband, a belt, a dog leash—you name it! Once you start finger weaving with T-yarn, you won't want to stop.

Here's what you need:
- **T-shirts without side seams or images**
- **ironing board**
- **fabric scissors**
- **needle and thread (optional)**

Step 1

Lay the T-shirt flat on an ironing board and cut off the bottom hem.

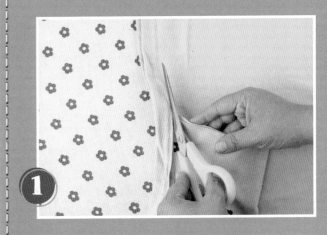

Step 2

Slide the T-shirt onto the narrow part of the ironing board like a tube. Make a diagonal cut from the bottom edge until you have about 1 inch in width. Begin cutting a strip of fabric about 1 inch wide all the way to the edge of the ironing board.

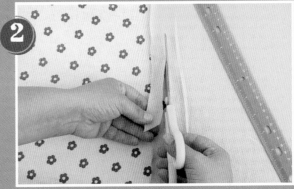

Step 3

Rotate the T-shirt on the ironing board and continue cutting the 1-inch strip. Continue rotating shirt and cutting in a spiral to make one long, continuous strip of fabric.

Step 4

When you reach the underarm seam, make another small diagonal cut to release the strip of fabric.

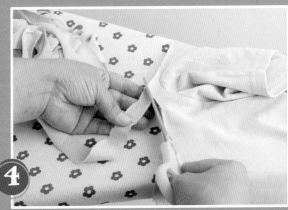

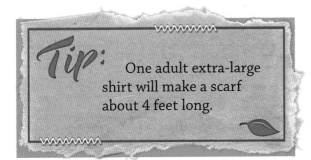

Tip: One adult extra-large shirt will make a scarf about 4 feet long.

To finish this project, turn to the next page. ⇨

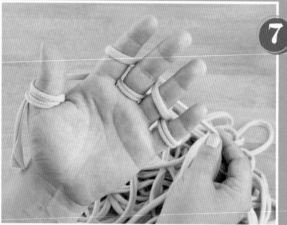

Step 5
Take about 1 foot of the strip in your hands and gently tug to stretch and curl the fabric. Work your way down the strip, pulling each 1-foot section.

Step 6 *(not pictured)*
Repeat steps 1 through 5 to make more T-yarn as needed.

Step 7
Wind the end of the T-yarn around your thumb two or three times. Weave the yarn through your fingers starting behind and ending in front of your index finger.

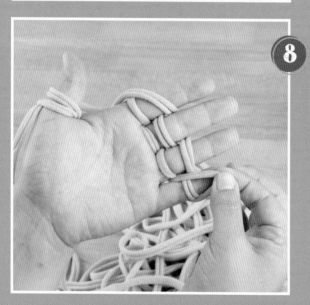

Step 8

Weave yarn around fingers again so you have two loops on each finger. Lift the bottom loops up, over, and off each finger to the back of your hand. You will have one loop left on each finger.

Step 9

Continue weaving and lifting off loops, occasionally tugging on the tube forming behind your hand. You can unwind the T-yarn from your thumb after you've lifted loops off your fingers a few times.

Step 10

When you reach the end of the yarn, you can attach more yarn by sewing the ends of two strips together.

Step 11

When the scarf is as long as you want it, cut the T-yarn, leaving a 6-inch tail. Thread the end through the remaining loops on your fingers and pull tight. Tuck the ends of the T-yarn inside the tube.

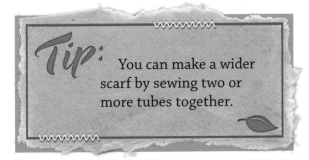

Tip: You can make a wider scarf by sewing two or more tubes together.

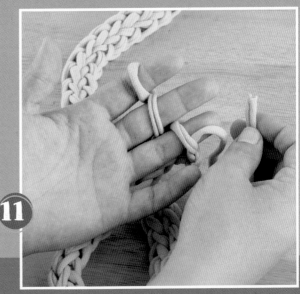

Pocket Purse

Lip gloss, MP3 player, notes from math class—you carry just about everything in your jeans pockets. Even if you've outgrown your jeans, you can still put those pockets to good use. By adding a shoulder strap and a little bit of fringe, your jeans pocket becomes a fashionable purse.

Here's what you need:
- fabric scissors
- old pair of jeans
- fabric glue
- pony beads
- needle and thread

Step 1
Cut out a back pocket from your jeans. Be sure to cut through both layers and leave the outside seams together.

Step 2
From a pant leg, cut a piece of jeans fabric into a 6-inch square. Cut the piece into ⅓-inch strips, leaving 1 inch at the top.

Step 3
Glue the jeans fringe on the back of the pocket. Cut off any fabric that hangs over the pocket edge.

Step 4
Thread a pony bead on the end of each piece of fringe.

Step 5
Cut the hems off both pant legs. Use a needle and thread to sew the two hems together. (See sewing instructions on page 19.)

Step 6
Sew the ends of the hems to the back of the pocket to form a shoulder strap.

Tip: Want a more colorful shoulder strap? A fabric belt works great. Just trim the belt to the length you want your strap. Then use a needle and thread to sew the belt to the pocket.

Pocket Magnet

Lockers can get crowded in a hurry with textbooks, binders, pencils, and backpacks. Get organized with some old jeans pockets. By adding a few magnets, pockets become a fun and functional way to organize your locker.

Step 1

Cut out the back pockets of your jeans. Be sure to cut through both layers and leave the outside seams together.

Step 2

Decorate the pockets with beads, buttons, or fabric paint.

Step 3

Hot glue a magnet to the back of the pocket.

Tip: This project only uses the pockets from an old pair of jeans. Save the remaining material to make other projects in this book.

How to Sew by Hand:

Slide the thread through the eye of the needle. Bring the ends of the thread together and tie a knot.

Poke your threaded needle through the fabric from underneath. Pull the thread through the fabric to knotted end. Poke your needle back through the fabric and up again to make a stitch. Continue weaving the needle in and out of the fabric, making small stitches in a straight line.

When you are finished sewing, make a loose stitch. Thread the needle through the loop and pull tight. Cut off remaining thread.

Wrist Wrap

Who needs diamonds when you have denim? With a few snips of the scissors, your jeans waistband can become a cool cuff bracelet. To make your cuff one-of-a-kind, just add ribbon or fabric paint.

Here's what you need:
- fabric scissors
- old pair of jeans
- glue gun and hot glue
- needle and thread
- ribbon or fabric paint (optional)

Step 1

Cut the waistband from a pair of jeans.

Step 2

Wrap the buttoned waistband around your wrist. Cut a length of the waistband about 1 inch longer than your wrist.

Step 3

On one end of the jeans material, cut the corners into a point.

Step 4

Hot glue both ends of the waistband together with the pointed end on top. Don't have a hot glue gun? Then sew the ends together with a needle and thread. (See sewing instructions on page 19.)

Tip: Belt loops are great for making matching rings. Just cut a belt loop off the waistband, and turn it inside out. Sew or hot glue the ends together.

T-bone

Got a pet that likes to chew? With T-shirt T-bones, even your pet pooch can go green. A tug toy made from old T-shirts is sure to be a hit with your dog or the dog next door. Just braid, knot, and get ready for some tug-of-war with man's best friend.

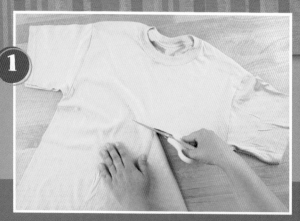

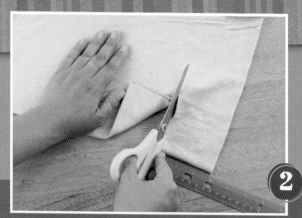

Step 1
Lay the T-shirt flat on a table or cutting surface. Cut off the bottom hem. Cut off the top of the shirt just below the underarm seam.

Step 2
Fold the T-shirt in half so the folded edges meet. Use a ruler to measure 3 inches from one cut edge. Cut across the fabric to make a 3-inch strip, making sure to cut through all layers.

Step 3
Unfold the strip. Cut off both side seams to make two strips. (If your T-shirt didn't have side seams, cut both ends of the loop.) Gently pull on the ends of each strip to stretch and curl the fabric.

Step 4 *(not pictured)*
Repeat steps 2 and 3 until you have 10 strips. Save the extra strip for another project. To add different colors to your braids, use T-shirts or scraps from other projects.

Step 5
Use masking tape to secure the ends of three strips to a table. Braid the strips tightly and secure both ends with masking tape. Repeat two more times.

Step 6
Hold all three braids together and tie a tight knot in one end. Tightly braid the three braids together and make another knot at the end. Remove the masking tape from the ends of the small braids.

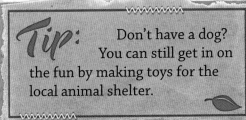

Tip: Don't have a dog? You can still get in on the fun by making toys for the local animal shelter.

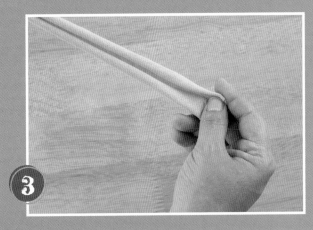

3

5

6

How to Braid
Lay three strips side by side. Cross the left strip over the middle strip to the center. Then cross the strip on the right over the new middle strip. Repeat, alternating left and right strips.

Hey Good Looking

Mirror, mirror on the wall, plus a place to store it all. This two-in-one project combines a mirror with a special spot to store your treasures. It's your own personal beauty center.

Here's what you need:
- fabric scissors
- old pair of jeans
- tape measure
- 12-inch by 18-inch piece of cardboard or matboard
- glue gun and hot glue
- mirror about 6 inches wide
- plastic gems or ribbon (optional)

Step 1
Cut off both pant legs about 6 inches from the end of the zipper.

Step 2
Cut along the seams of both pant legs to create flat pieces of jeans material.

Step 3
Turn material rightside down and lay cardboard on top. Fold material over the edges to make sure it fits.

Step 4
Hot glue the edges of the material to the backside of the cardboard. Cut off any extra material.

To finish this project, turn to the next page. ⇨

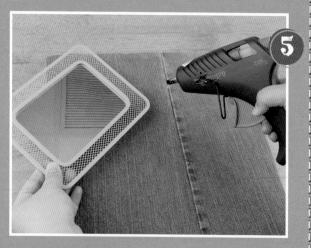

Step 5
Hot glue the mirror onto the front of the jeans-covered cardboard, about 2 inches from the top. Set aside.

Step 6
Cut front of jeans from the inseam to the waistband.

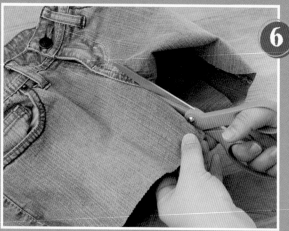

Step 7
Cut along the center back seam from the inseam to the waistband. When you are finished cutting, you should have a panel with a front and back pocket.

Step 8
Place the pocket panel near the bottom of the cardboard piece so that the material folds over the bottom edge.

Step 9
Wrap the panel around the bottom and sides of the cardboard. Hot glue the panel to the back of the cardboard.

Step 10
Use the second pant leg to cover the back. Cut a section about 11 inches by 18 inches. Hot glue this section to the back of the cardboard.

Optional
Decorate with plastic gems or ribbon.

Old Clothes Crafting Facts

● Denim jeans and many T-shirts are made of cotton, a natural fiber. Natural fibers are biodegradable, which means they will break down in a landfill. T-shirts made of a cotton and polyester blend don't break down as easily.

● Cotton crops use 25 percent of the world's pesticides. To reduce your impact on the environment, look for jeans made with organic cotton. Organic cotton is grown without the use of harsh chemicals.

● When printed T-shirts end up in a landfill, they present a large problem. Many of the inks used are bad for the environment. Eventually the inks pollute the soil or flow into rivers and streams.

● Many nonprofit thrift stores accept old T-shirts and jeans as long as they are in usable condition. They sell the items to the public. The money from the sales goes to help people in need.

🐞 When thrift stores receive T-shirts that are too worn-out to resell, they send them to rag sorters. The rag sorters recycle cotton T-shirts into wiping and polishing cloths.

🐞 What can you do with all the scraps from your jeans and T-shirt projects? That is, of course, if you're not saving the scraps for future use. Call your local recycling center to find out if cotton material is accepted. If not, they may be able to help you find a fabric recycler near you.

Recyclables

Every day people all over the world do their part to help the environment. You've probably been recycling at home or at school for years. But did you know simple crafts can also help the environment? You can keep CDs, cans, bottles, and wrappers out of the landfill and have fun too. With a little creativity, you can turn them into candleholders, coasters, jewelry, and other fun projects.

Reusing CDs, cans, bottles, and wrappers has become a new art form. These creative crafts help to spread the word about the importance of recycling. Wrappers, plastic bottles, and cans keep your food fresh and safe to eat. But these items are also the most common type of litter found along highways and in nature areas. Not many people realize that these items can be reused in creative ways. Once you start thinking about reusing, you'll be amazed by how many ideas you'll come up with. Recycled, reused, repurposed, restyled—whatever you call it, you'll be doing your part to help the environment.

Good News

Aluminum cans are the most commonly used beverage container, and they're 100 percent recyclable. About half of all cans used are recycled, but that's still good news. Recycling aluminum creates less water and air pollution than making new cans. And recycling uses about 95 percent less energy than creating aluminum from raw materials.

CD Safety

Some music CDs have a protective layer that makes them thicker and harder to cut. When possible, use burnable discs for projects that involve cutting CDs. They are thinner and easier to cut.

Remember to wear safety glasses to protect your eyes when cutting CDs. You may also want to wear gardening gloves when handling sharp CD pieces.

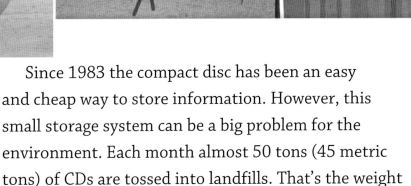

Since 1983 the compact disc has been an easy and cheap way to store information. However, this small storage system can be a big problem for the environment. Each month almost 50 tons (45 metric tons) of CDs are tossed into landfills. That's the weight of a herd of elephants!

Solving an environmental problem this big calls for lots of creative thinking. Rather than tossing your scratched CDs in the trash, recycle them into something new. Even the cases can be turned into stylish photo frames. Let's get started!

Tool Tidy

Crafty kids know that staying organized is a must. Clean up your space with a craft caddy made from old tin cans. Just use a little paint and colorful yarn to recycle tin cans into stylish containers. Make the caddy as large or small as you need. After all, your craft space should be as unique as the projects you make there.

Here's what you need:
- newspaper
- tin cans, clean
- spray paint, for metal
- yarn
- glue gun and hot glue
- scissors

XXXX

XXXX

1

Step 1
Lay old newspapers on the ground outside or in an open space. Place the cans on the newspaper and spray paint the cans. Make sure to read and follow the instructions and safety precautions on the spray paint can. Let cans dry completely.

Step 2
Begin wrapping yarn around the can. You can start at the very top or leave some of the can showing. Overlap the end of the yarn tightly to hold in place.

Step 3
Continue wrapping the can in yarn, placing strands close together so the can doesn't show through. When you've covered as much of the can as you want, cut the yarn.

Step 4
Hot glue the yarn end in place. Repeat steps 2 through 4 with all of the cans.

Step 5
Arrange the cans, making sure the glued ends of yarn do not show. Hot glue the cans together.

Tip: The inside cut edge of tin cans can be very sharp. Use care when cleaning and handling the cans.

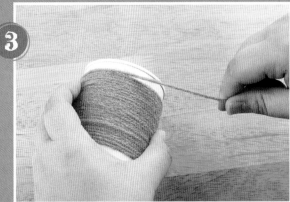

You've Been Framed

Old CDs are great for craft projects, but the reusing doesn't stop there. After all, even the packaging can be recycled into something new. A shiny CD border turns a plastic CD case into a cool stand-up frame.

Here's what you need:
- CD case
- scissors
- 1 or 2 CDs
- tacky glue
- transparent tape

1

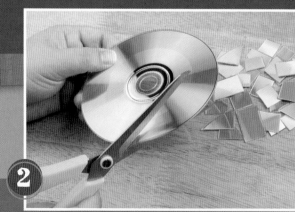

2

Step 1
Remove the paper from inside the CD case.

Step 2
Cut CDs into small squares.

Step 3
Glue the CD pieces around the outside edges of the case's front cover.

Step 4
Tape your photo to the inside of the case.

Step 5 (*not pictured*)
Carefully separate the front of the case from the back of the case. Be careful not to break the plastic tabs.

Step 6
Flip the bottom cover upside down. Reattach the top and bottom of the case.

CD SAFETY!
Safety glasses should be worn when cutting CDs. Sharp pieces can fly up.

Itty Bitty Frames

Everyone knows you can recycle glass soda bottles. But what about the metal caps? Instead of throwing them away, turn bottle caps into something artistic and useful. Adding pictures to bottle caps is an easy way to make fun magnets for your locker. Make plenty of these little frames to share with your friends.

Here's what you need:

- bottle cap
- magazine
- pen
- scissors
- cardstock or other heavy paper
- clear glue
- clear tape
- superglue
- toothpick
- thin, self-adhesive magnets

1

2

Step 1
Place a bottle cap on a small picture in a magazine. Trace around the cap with a pen, and cut out the picture.

Step 2
Trace the bottle cap onto a piece of cardstock and cut out the circle. Spread a small drop of glue on one side of the circle. Press the picture to the cardstock circle and let dry.

Step 3
Cover the front of the picture with clear tape, making sure not to leave any gaps. The tape will keep the glue in step 5 from soaking into the paper. Trim off extra tape.

Step 4
Carefully apply small drops of superglue to the raised circle inside the bottle cap. Be careful not to touch the glue with your fingers. Press the picture into the cap. Allow the superglue to dry.

Step 5
Put a small amount of clear glue on the picture. Tilt the bottle cap around to spread the glue over the whole picture. If air bubbles form, use a toothpick to move the glue around. Let dry completely.

Step 6
Peel off the adhesive liner from the back of a thin magnet. Press the magnet to the back of the bottle cap frame.

Tip: You can also use photos of your friends or pets for this project. Use a computer to resize your images so they're small enough to fit inside the bottle caps. Then print the photos on photo paper.

3

4

5

6

Mosaic Flowerpot

Brighten your backyard with a mosaic flowerpot made with old CDs. Flowerpots placed throughout the garden add interest and color. Bits of broken CDs create a mirrored surface that reflects sunlight and makes your plants sparkle.

Here's what you need:

- scissors
- 3 CDs
- glue gun and hot glue
- 4 ½-inch flowerpot
- glass gems

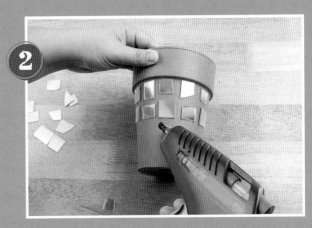

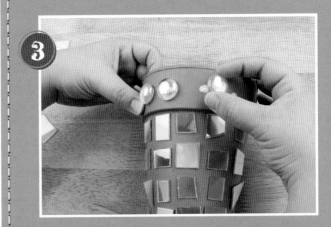

Step 1
Cut the CDs into small pieces.

Step 2
Hot glue the CD pieces onto the flowerpot. Leave a small space between each piece.

Step 3
Hot glue gems along the top edge of the pot. Allow the glue to dry before adding dirt and flowers.

Sweet Boxes

What's better than a gift of sweet treats? Giving them in special sweet boxes made by you! With a few candy wrappers and some decoupage glue, you can make these special gift boxes. With so many candy choices, each box will be a sweet treat!

Here's what you need:
- candy wrappers
- scissors
- small cardboard box with lid
- newspaper
- small sponge brush
- decoupage glue

xxxx

Step 1 *(not pictured)*
Trim off any parts of the wrappers that you don't want to show, such as the ingredient list.

Step 2
Place a small cardboard box and lid on old newspapers. Using a small sponge brush, cover the back of one wrapper with decoupage glue.

Step 3
Lay the wrapper flat on the box. Smooth out any wrinkles with your fingers. Cover the top of the wrapper and the surrounding area with decoupage glue.

Step 4 *(not pictured)*
Repeat steps 2 and 3 until the box and lid are covered with wrappers. Let dry.

Step 5
Apply a thin layer of decoupage glue over the whole box and lid. Let box and lid dry completely before placing the lid on the box.

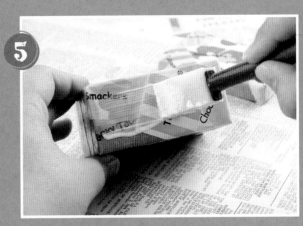

Tip: You can use decoupage to cover other things, such as notebooks or folders.

Cuff 'em

Covered with your favorite yarn, an ordinary soda can becomes something fun and stylish. No one will guess that you made this bracelet from something out of the recycle bin. And they're so easy to make, you can make one to match every outfit.

Here's what you need:
- gardening gloves
- scissors
- aluminum can
- white glue
- yarn
- needle and thread
- 1 snap

Step 1
Wearing gardening gloves for safety, cut a 2-inch wide strip from the center of an aluminum can. Trim the ends so they are slightly rounded with no sharp points.

Step 2
Apply a thin layer of white glue to one-fourth of the bracelet on both front and back sides. Use your finger to smear the glue so the first one-fourth of both sides are covered.

Step 3
Lay about 1 inch of yarn horizontally on the back of the bracelet. Press the yarn down so it sticks to glue.

Step 4
Wind the yarn around the bracelet, overlapping the end piece and pressing the yarn into the glue. Place the strands close together so metal doesn't show through.

Step 5 *(not pictured)*
Working in sections, apply glue and wrap the bracelet with yarn as in steps 2 and 4.

Step 6
Cut the yarn leaving a 2-inch tail. Apply a narrow strip of glue on the back side of the bracelet and press the end of the yarn down. Let dry completely.

Step 7
Use a needle and thread to sew the front and back of a snap to opposite ends of the bracelet. Line up both parts of the snap so bracelet is even when worn.

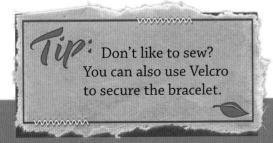

Tip: Don't like to sew? You can also use Velcro to secure the bracelet.

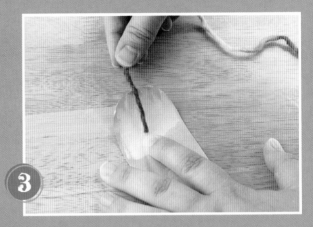

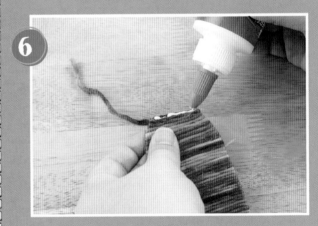

Stick 'em Up

Turn your locker from drab to fab in just a few minutes. All it takes are a couple of CD magnets and some of your favorite photos. Before long your friends will be begging you to help them make their own.

Here's what you need:
- all-purpose glue
- 2 CDs
- tape measure
- thin, self-adhesive magnet strips
- scissors
- permanent markers

Step 1
Glue the lower halves of two CDs together with the shiny sides facing out.

Step 2
Use a tape measure to mark off two 2-inch strips of magnet. Cut magnet strips.

Step 3
Peel the backing off the magnet strips and attach to the top and bottom of one CD.

Optional
Use permanent markers to add fun designs to the CD magnet.

Tip: Instead of buying magnetic strips, just look around your home. Reusing an old magnet is a great way to save on supplies.

Candy Lover's Ring

Looking for a ring to jazz up a new outfit? If you also have a sweet tooth, this project is for you! Show your love for your favorite candy by making a sweet ring from the leftover wrappers. A little folding and weaving is all it takes to make a one-of-a-kind ring.

Here's what you need:
- candy wrappers, cut to about 1 ¾ inches by 2 ½ inches

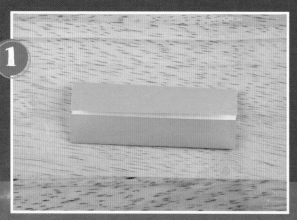

1

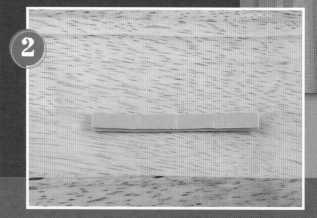

2

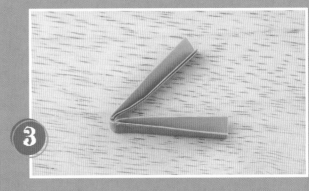

Step 1
Place one wrapper on a flat surface with the colored side down. Fold both long edges to middle.

Step 2
Fold the wrapper in half lengthwise two times. The folded wrapper will be about ¼ inch wide.

Step 3
Fold wrapper in half the other way.

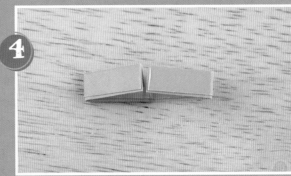

Step 4
Fold both short edges in to the middle crease. Repeat steps 1 through 4 with another wrapper.

Step 5
Turn the wrappers on their sides so only the folded edges show. Insert points 1 and 2 of second wrapper into openings A and B of first wrapper.

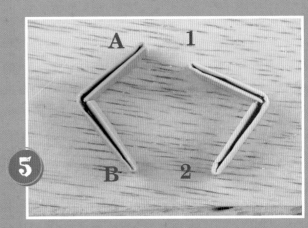

Step 6
Pull second wrapper through. Be sure the folded edge of second wrapper is on the left.

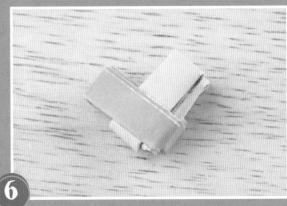

To finish this project, turn to the next page. ⇨

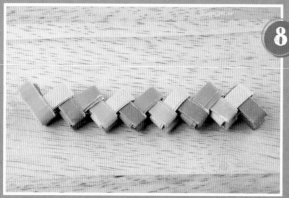

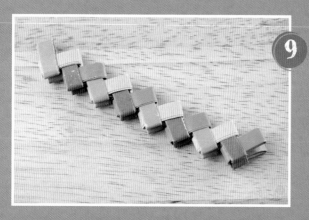

Step 7

Fold a third wrapper as directed in steps 1 through 4. Insert third wrapper from top to bottom into openings of second wrapper as in step 5. Pull through, making sure folded edge of third wrapper is on the left.

Step 8

Continue folding and weaving wrappers together until the chain is just long enough to wrap around your finger. End with an odd number of links.

Step 9

Fold one more wrapper as in steps 1 through 4. Insert into chain as before but with folded edge on the right instead of the left.

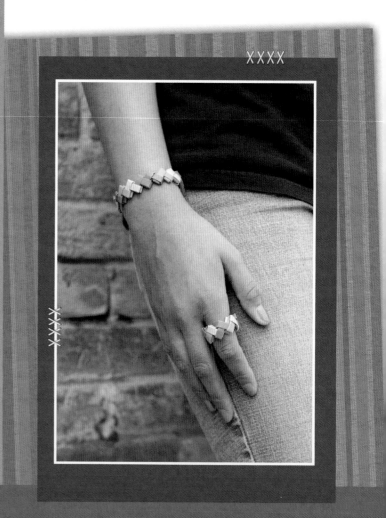

Step 10
Bend the chain into a ring. Lift the outer layer of the first wrapper in chain so the ends of the wrapper are showing.

Step 11
Insert the ends of the first wrapper into the folded edge openings of the last wrapper.

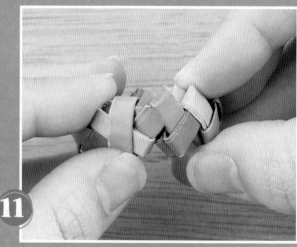

Step 12
Slide the outer layer of the first wrapper back into place, covering the last wrapper.

Tip: Once you've learned how to make the wrapper chain, you can make a bracelet, necklace, belt, or headband. If you're up for a challenge, you can sew several chains together to make a coin purse.

Lighten Up

Light up the night and go green with a candleholder made from an empty tin can. Tin can luminaries are easy to make and beautiful when lit. Make snowflake designs for Christmas, stars for the Fourth of July, or create any design you like. Make one to dress up a table or a whole group for the porch or patio. After all, the cans are free!

Here's what you need:

- **tin can, clean**
- **permanent marker**
- **water**
- **freezer**
- **hammer**
- **towel**
- **large nail**
- **newspaper**
- **spray paint, for metal**
- **tea light candle**

Step 1
Use a permanent marker to draw a design on the outside of a tin can.

Step 2 *(not pictured)*
Fill the can nearly to the top with water and freeze. If the bottom of the can bulges during freezing, you can use a hammer to flatten it out after step 4.

Step 3
Place the can on its side on a hard surface covered by a towel. Use a hammer and a large nail to tap holes through the can following your design.

Step 4 *(not pictured)*
Place the can in the sink until the ice melts.

Step 5
When the can is dry, take it outside or to an open space. Set the can on old newspapers and spray paint it. Make sure to follow the instructions and safety precautions on the spray paint can. Let can dry completely. Now you are ready to add a tea light candle.

Tip: Depending on how it's opened, a tin can may have a sharp top edge. Be very careful when handling the can.

Party Coasters

Everyone knows CDs with the latest tunes will get your party rocking. But did you know CDs can add sparkle to your table too? Just hand your guests CD coasters along with their drinks.

Here's what you need:
- 1 CD
- piece of felt at least 5 inches by 5 inches
- permanent marker
- scissors
- all-purpose glue
- small plastic gems

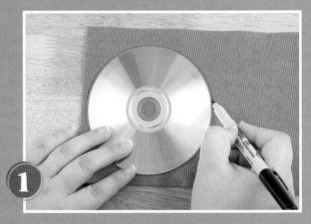

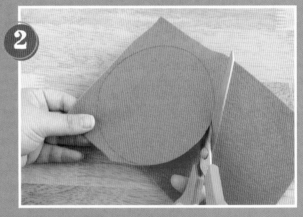

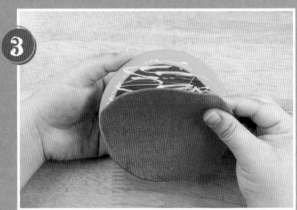

Step 1
Place a CD onto a piece of felt. Trace around the CD with a marker.

Step 2
Cut out the felt circle.

Step 3
Glue the felt onto the label side of the CD.

Step 4
Glue plastic gems around the outside edge of the CD.

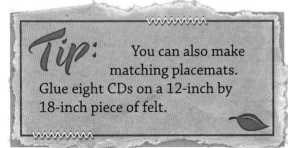

Tip: You can also make matching placemats. Glue eight CDs on a 12-inch by 18-inch piece of felt.

Green Crafting Facts

Tin cans are made mostly of steel. A thin coating of tin inside the can protects the food's flavor and keeps the can from rusting. About 63 percent of tin cans are recycled, making them one of the most recycled products in America.

Many beverage cans are made from aluminum. On average, people in the United States use one aluminum can every day. About 18 million cans are recycled in the United States each year. That amount is just over half of the cans used.

Many artists have started using aluminum cans in their work. Because aluminum is light and flexible, it has become a popular choice for jewelry. Even pop tabs can become works of art in the right hands. Some artists have designed clothing and hats made from these little aluminum pieces.

🐞 CDs are considered class 7 recyclables. Class 7 plastics are the hardest to recycle. When CDs are recycled, they are used to make auto parts, street lights, and office equipment.

🐞 Scientists believe it will take more than 1 million years for a CD to completely break down in a landfill.

🐞 Water is good for everyone, but plastic bottles are not. It takes about 700 years for one plastic bottle to begin breaking down. About 38 billion plastic water bottles are thrown away every year. All those bottles will be taking up landfill space for a long time.

All Natural

For awesome art supplies, you don't need to go far. Thanks to Mother Nature, many supplies can be found in your own backyard! From flowers to leaves to twigs, a little gathering on your part can go a long way. Using natural items for crafts isn't just inexpensive. It's also a great way to reuse Earth's materials and let them live on for a lot longer. Now that's music to our eco-friendly ears!

Reusing flowers, leaves, and twigs also helps cut down on waste. That's a great green move because yard waste takes up a lot of valuable landfill space. Instead, create crafts that are chock-full of earthy appeal. Once you dig in, your creativity is sure to bloom and grow.

Did You Know?

Composting is another way to cut down on yard waste. Collect leaves, grass clippings, pine needles, and more in a compost bin. By doing so, you'll help feed the earth and save the planet too. Composting creates healthy garden soil and keeps yard waste out of landfills. It's a win-win for everyone!

Saving the planet can seem overwhelming. But reusing materials to make crafts is a small step that can make a big difference. Give new life to beans, seeds, and cones, and plant the seeds for a greener world at the same time! After all, even little steps—and crafts—add up to one big change for Earth.

Simple items from your backyard or pantry are all you need for cool crafts. Get ready to have some fun. After all, making eco-friendly art isn't just good for the planet—it's also a good time!

Terrific Twigs

This stylish vase just might steal the show from the flowers. Made using twigs, this nature vase isn't just a nifty decoration. It's extra eco-friendly because you can reuse a glass jar too.

Here's what you need:

- glass jar, clean
- ruler
- wire snips
- twigs, ¼-inch thick
- glue gun and hot glue
- ribbon, ¾-inch wide

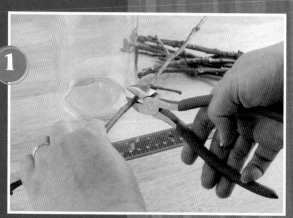

1

2

Step 1
Measure the height of a jar with a ruler. Have an adult use wire snips to cut twigs to 1 inch longer than the jar.

Step 2
Apply a thin line of hot glue to one twig.

Step 3
Press the twig onto the jar. Hold the twig in place for about 15 seconds.

Step 4
Repeat steps 2 and 3 until the jar is covered with twigs. Be sure to place each twig close to the previous one so the jar doesn't show.

Step 5
Tie a ribbon around the middle of the vase.

Step 6
Hot glue the ribbon in place.

Tip: For a striped vase, paint the twigs different colors before gluing them to the jar. Set it off with a bright ribbon to make multicolored magic!

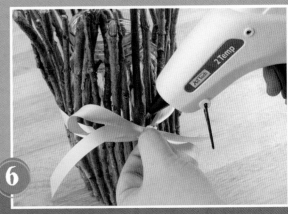

59

Dream On

According to some American Indian traditions, dream catchers trap your dreams in their weblike patterns. The dreams spin around the web, and only good ones make it through. Ward off nasty nightmares with this darling dream catcher. Simply hang it above your bed and get ready for sweet dreams.

Here's what you need:
- 1 flexible willow twig, about 3 feet long
- thin wire
- scissors
- dental floss
- 1 large bead
- 3 pieces of thin twine, about 6 inches long
- 3 feathers

Step 1
Gently bend a twig into a hoop. Fasten the ends together with a piece of thin wire.

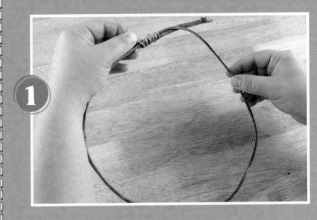

Step 2
Cut a piece of dental floss to be about five times the length of your arm. Knot one end of the floss to the top of the hoop. Snip off the short end of the floss.

Step 3
Make six evenly spaced half-hitch knots around the hoop in a clockwise direction. Keep the floss tight as you work, being careful not to change the shape of the hoop.

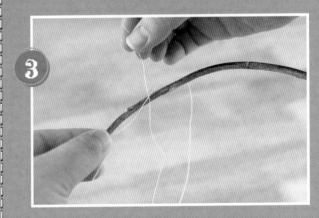

Step 4
Make another row of the web by making half-hitch knots in the centers of the open loops of the previous row.

How to make a half-hitch knot:
Loop the dental floss over the twig from the front, or the side facing you, to the back. Pull the end of the floss back to the front through the loop you've just made.

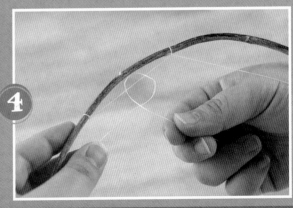

To finish this project, turn to the next page.

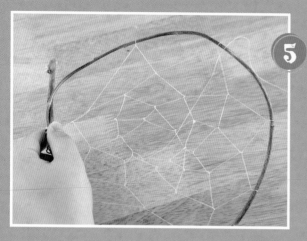

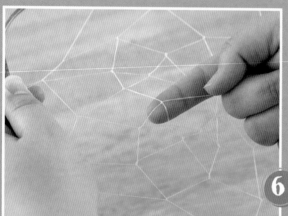

Step 5

Continue adding rows to the web until you are left with a small circle in the center of the web.

Step 6

Tie a knot in the floss close to the last half-hitch knot.

Step 7

Thread the end of the floss through a large bead. Pull the bead close to the knot you made in step 6. Then make another knot in the floss to keep the bead in place. Snip off the end of the floss.

Step 8
Tie a piece of thin twine to the bottom of the dream catcher. Snip off the short end of the twine.

Step 9
Tie the other end of the twine to a feather.

Step 10
Repeat steps 8 and 9 two more times, placing the twine to the left and right of the first piece.

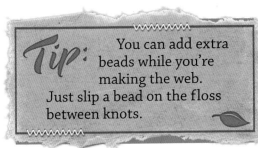

Tip: You can add extra beads while you're making the web. Just slip a bead on the floss between knots.

8

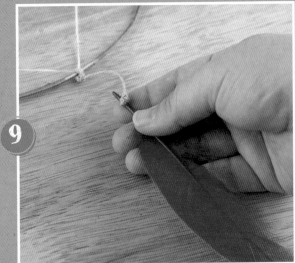

9

10

Picture This

Think outside the box and use beans instead of paint for your next masterpiece. Beans come in a wide variety of colors, shapes, and sizes. Using them to make a mosaic is a great way to show them off. Anything from soup beans to kidney beans to black beans will do. By mixing colorful beans and creativity, the results are cool as can be!

Here's what you need:
- hole puncher
- clear plastic lid, round, at least 6 inches wide
- pencil
- white paper
- dried beans, assorted colors
- craft glue
- small paintbrush
- ribbon, ½-inch to ¾-inch wide, about 1 foot long

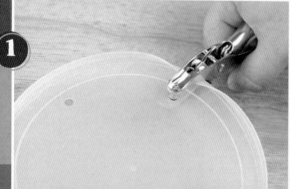

1

2

Step 1
Punch two holes through a clear plastic lid as if at 11 and 1 on a clock. Avoid gluing beans over these holes in steps 4 and 5.

Step 2
Trace the lid on white paper. In the circle, draw a simple design or image to use as the guide for your mosaic.

Step 3
Place the drawing under the plastic lid. Select a section of the picture that will be all the same color. Pick out the beans you want to use for this section.

Step 4
Using the drawing as a guide, apply glue onto the lid over the chosen section with a small paintbrush.

Step 5
Press the beans onto the glue. Be sure to place the beans close together so the plastic doesn't show through.

Step 6 *(not pictured)*
Continue applying glue and adding beans section by section until the entire picture is filled in. Let dry for one week.

Step 7
Thread ribbon through the holes in the lid. Tie ribbon at the top for hanging.

Tip: Stumped for what to draw? Flip through your favorite magazine for ideas.

Bottle It Up

Regular vases are oh-so-yesterday. Transform a boring bottle into a stylish vase bursting with floral finesse. By using colorful beans and a pattern of your choosing, you'll have a one-of-a-kind vase. Add colorful daisies or sassy sunflowers to truly brighten your space.

Here's what you need:

- measuring cup with pour spout
- dried beans, various colors and sizes
- clear glass beverage bottle with wide mouth, clean and label removed
- fake flowers
- ribbon, ½-inch wide

Step 1
Use a measuring cup to pour a layer of beans about 1 inch deep into a glass bottle. Tap the bottom of the bottle on a table to pack the beans in tightly.

Step 2
Add another layer of beans using a different kind of bean. Smaller or larger layers will create various-sized stripes.

Step 3
Continue adding layers of beans and tapping the bottom until the bottle is full.

Step 4
Arrange fake flowers in the vase by poking them into the beans.

Step 5
Tie a ribbon around the neck of the bottle.

Tip: You can also add glitter or sand in with the beans to spice up the look.

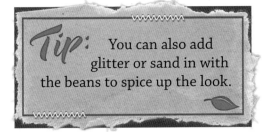

Forest Frame

Branch out with an entirely different kind of photo frame! This forest-inspired frame adds a touch of woodsy wonder to any wall. Once you collect your twiggy tools, you'll have a blast framing the day away.

Here's what you need:
- wire snips
- 12 twigs, about ¼-inch thick
- ruler
- craft glue
- 4-inch by 6-inch photo
- cardboard, cut to 6 inches wide by 8 inches long
- glue gun and hot glue
- 4 acorns (optional)
- ribbon, ¼-inch wide, 6 inches long

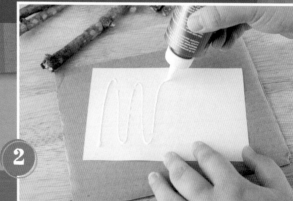

Step 1
Have an adult use wire snips to cut six twigs to 9 inches long. Have the adult cut another six twigs to 7 inches long.

Step 2
Use craft glue to attach a photo to the center of the cardboard.

Step 3
Lay the twigs around the photo to see how they will fit. The longer twigs will be glued across the top and bottom. The shorter twigs will be glued along the sides.

Step 4
Once you have a layout you like, hot glue the twigs in place one at a time. Be sure to cover all the cardboard.

Step 5 *(optional)*
For a decorative touch, hot glue an acorn to each corner of the frame.

Step 6
Hot glue one end of a ribbon to the backside of the frame at the top left corner. Hot glue the other end to the backside at the top right corner to make a loop for hanging.

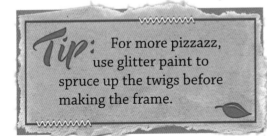

Tip: For more pizzazz, use glitter paint to spruce up the twigs before making the frame.

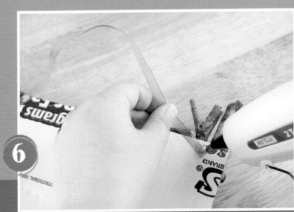

Fresh and Bright

Pinecones don't just smell pretty—they look pretty too! Show them off in this sweet-smelling night-light. This craft lets you capture that great outdoors smell in your home all year long.

Here's what you need:
- ½ cup water
- spray bottle
- pine essential oil
- small pinecones, about 60
- plastic zipper-seal bag, gallon size
- twinkle lights, strand of 50 lights
- clear tape
- clear glass jar, 4-quart size

Step 1
Put water into a spray bottle. Add seven drops of essential oil.

Step 2
Place pinecones in the sink and spray them with the water and oil. Seal the pinecones in a plastic bag and let sit for 24 hours.

Step 3
Plug in the string of lights. Leaving enough cord to reach the outlet, tape the light string to the outside of a clear glass jar near the bottom.

Step 4
Run the string of lights up to the top of the jar. Tape the cord between the lights in a few places so that the cord stays attached to the jar.

Step 5
Using the other end of the light string, make a circle around the inside bottom of the jar.

Step 6
Add a layer of pinecones into the jar. Then make another circle with the lights.

Step 7 *(not pictured)*
Repeat steps 5 and 6 until the jar is full.

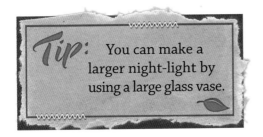

Tip: You can make a larger night-light by using a large glass vase.

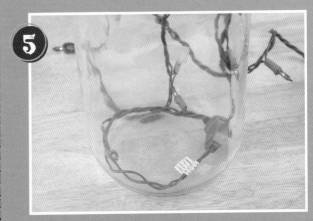

Here Birdy, Birdy!

If you think you know all there is to know about pinecone bird feeders, think again. Load up this pinecone garland with peanut butter and bird snacks and—voila! Dinner for birds is served. No doubt, all the birds will be flocking to your yard!

Here's what you need:
- wire snips
- floral wire, about 8 feet
- ruler
- 12 pinecones, various types and sizes
- jute twine, about 3½ feet
- newspaper
- spoon
- 1 cup smooth peanut butter
- 1 cup birdseed
- ½ cup raisins, soaked in water to soften

Step 1
Have an adult use wire snips to cut floral wire into 12 8-inch pieces.

Step 2
Wrap one wire around a pinecone at the base, tucking the wire inside the pinecone's scales. Twist the ends of the wire together leaving a long tail. Repeat with all pinecones.

Step 3
Lay a piece of jute on a table or counter covered in newspaper. Arrange the wired pinecones along the sides of the jute, alternating large and small pinecones. Leave about 10 inches of jute on one end without pinecones.

Step 4
Attach pinecones to the jute by tightly winding the wire tails around the jute. Twist the wire back on itself to secure. Tuck in the end so no sharp points are left.

Step 5
Use a spoon to spread peanut butter on the pinecones, covering the top of each scale.

Step 6
Sprinkle birdseed over the pinecones. Press raisins onto some of the scales. Let sit for 24 hours to harden.

Step 7
Hang the bird feeder from a tree by tying the end of the jute without pinecones around a branch.

Tip: Try adding cracked corn, sunflower seeds, and berries to the pinecones. Some birds even enjoy a treat of grape or strawberry jelly.

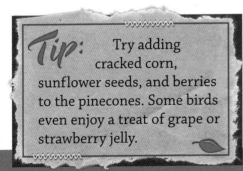

Gorgeous Gifts

When you get a gift, it's tempting to quickly tear open the box. Yet with these great gift boxes, your friends may just stare at the lovely designs you've created. They'll barely be able to contain themselves after receiving one of these cute containers!

Here's what you need:
- small cardboard box with lid
- newspaper
- acrylic paint, any color
- 2 small paintbrushes
- white colored pencil
- tacky glue
- seeds and beans in a variety of colors
- 1 tablespoon water
- small bowl

1

2

Step 1
Place a small cardboard box and lid on newspaper. Paint the entire outside of the box and lid. Let dry.

Step 2
Place the lid on the box. Use a white colored pencil to trace a line around the box at the bottom edge of the lid.

Step 3
Lightly draw out simple patterns, such as stripes or triangles, on each side of the box and lid. Avoid the top edge of the box that will be covered by the lid.

Step 4
Use a clean paintbrush to apply a thick layer of tacky glue to one section of a design on the box.

Step 5
Press your choice of beans or seeds over the glue. Try to place the seeds or beans close together so the box doesn't show through.

Step 6 *(not pictured)*
Working on one section at a time, repeat steps 4 and 5 until the entire box and lid are covered.

Step 7
Mix 1 tablespoon glue and 1 tablespoon water in a small bowl. Use the paintbrush to apply glue mixture over entire box and lid. Allow to dry overnight.

Tip: For a more casual look, mix the beans and seeds together on a plate. Cover one surface of the box or lid in glue and press into the seeds. Repeat with all sides of the box and lid.

All Natural Crafting Facts

🐞 Since ancient times, people have used natural products to beautify their skin. Today you can hit the pantry to see what nature has to offer. Try mixing ¼ cup each of honey and flax seed for a rich facial scrub. Leave on for 10 minutes, and don't forget to thank Mother Nature!

🐞 Want another great way to use seeds to help the environment? Consider writing letters and invitations on seed paper. After it's read this paper can be buried in the garden and grown into wildflowers. Talk about recycling at its finest!

🐞 If you love to watch birds, plant sunflowers in your yard. A sunflower makes a beautiful, all-natural bird feeder. Plant sunflowers in full sun where you can see them through a window or from a patio. It won't be long before feathered friends stop by.

Don't just hug a tree, plant one! Trees do lots of good for the environment. They help reduce pollution by absorbing carbon dioxide and cut down on global warming. Plus, we couldn't make such cool crafts without 'em!

Go, go, H_2O! Everyone runs water to warm it up before a shower. Put a bucket under the tub faucet to collect that wasted water. After your shower use that water to keep your plants and flowers bloomin' fresh.

Paper and Cardboard

Believe it or not, you'll probably use about 18 tons (16 metric tons) of paper in your lifetime. You will also likely receive 560 pieces of junk mail every year. And that's not counting all those fashion magazines piling up in your room! If that sounds like a lot of wasted paper, you're right. But there's good news too. By reusing materials you can make a big difference to the environment. And the great news is that being green can be fun!

Get ready to get creative because soon you'll be turning old paper into new, cool crafts. You won't be just keeping paper out of the landfill. You'll be making useful and attractive items of which you can be proud. Talk about turning trash into treasures!

Pretty presentation is a big part of what makes giving gifts fun. Wrapping paper is a great way to dress up packages. But boxes and wrappings are often tossed aside when we're happily enjoying our gifts. The bad news is that all the extra waste can really take its toll on the environment.

Luckily, going green doesn't have to mean a lifetime of plain-looking gifts. Wrapping paper and cardboard can be reused in new ways. From awesome accessories to darling display items, recycled crafts are gifts you can give yourself for free. Soon you'll be dreaming up more green gifts and making art all year long.

Did You Know?

Keeping paper out of the landfill is important, but there are other benefits to recycling. Recycling uses less energy than it takes to make paper from raw materials. As a result the process produces less air pollution. And 1 ton of recycled paper saves 17 trees.

Boho Beads

If you love that earthy boho look, then these chunky paper beads are a perfect style fit! String them together to make bracelets, necklaces, and other fun accessories. But be warned—people might stop you on the street. They'll want to know where you got your fabulous jewelry!

Here's what you need:
- newspaper, 2 sheets
- large mixing bowl
- boiling water
- 2 tablespoons white glue
- toothpicks
- cookie sheet
- wax paper
- acrylic paint
- clear gloss sealer spray
- ribbon, ¼-inch wide
- clear tape

Step 1

Rip newspaper into tiny pieces. Put the pieces into a large mixing bowl.

Step 2

Have an adult pour 1 cup boiling water over the newspaper in the bowl. Let the water cool for one hour, stirring every 10 minutes.

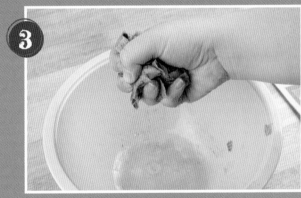

Step 3

Slowly pour out excess water from the paper. Squeeze the paper to remove as much water as possible and drain again.

Step 4

Add white glue to the paper. Mix with your hands until the paper sticks together in a large ball.

To finish this project, turn to the next page.

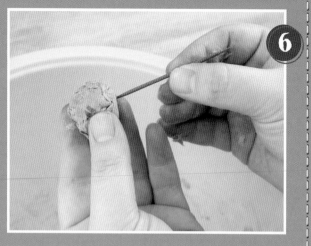

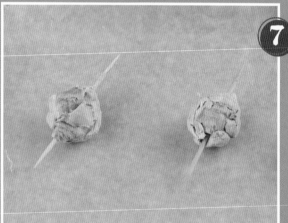

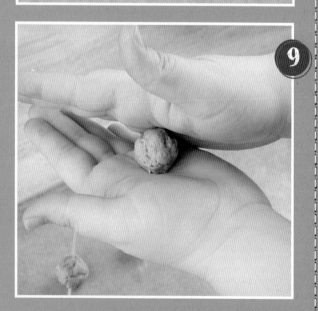

Step 5 *(not pictured)*

Roll the paper into round beads of any size. If needed, add more glue to help the beads stick together better.

Step 6

Use a toothpick to poke a hole through one bead. Leave the toothpick in the bead.

Step 7

Place the bead on a cookie sheet covered with wax paper.

Step 8 *(not pictured)*

Repeat steps 6 and 7 with all beads.

Step 9

Allow the beads to dry for one week. Roll the beads between your palms three to four times each day so they don't develop a flat side.

Step 10

When the beads are completely dry, use acrylic or metallic paint to color the beads. Let paint dry.

Step 11

Take the beads outside and set them on newspaper. Spray with clear gloss sealer following the directions and safety tips on the can. Allow the beads to dry before removing the toothpicks.

Step 12

Roll one end of a piece of ribbon into a point. Use a small piece of clear tape to secure the end. Thread beads onto the ribbon, adding small knots between each bead. When enough beads are strung to make a bracelet or necklace, tie the ends of the ribbon in a knot and trim ends.

Tip: For a multicolored look, apply two coats of paint in different colors. When the second coat is dry, use sandpaper to create a fun two-toned effect.

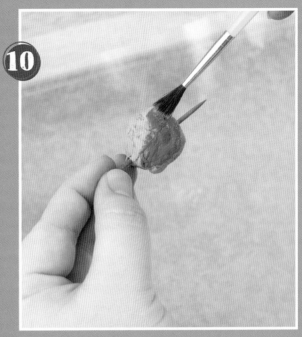

Jazzy Journal

Why spend your money on a fancy journal when you can make one at home? This project turns a plain composition book into the jazziest journal around. There's just one problem. It's so cute, you won't want to keep it a secret!

Here's what you need:
- ruler
- scissors
- magazines
- glue stick
- toothpick
- photo, cut to 4 inches by 3 inches
- craft glue
- composition notebook

Step 1
Measure and cut 106 squares of colorful magazine paper about 3 inches square.

Step 2
Use a glue stick to apply glue diagonally from corner to corner on the back side of one square.

Step 3
Starting at one glued corner, tightly roll the square around a toothpick to form a tiny tube. Hold the end down for a few seconds to secure. Snip a bit off the ends of the tube so that they are flat.

Step 4 *(not pictured)*
Repeat steps 2 and 3 with all of the magazine pieces.

Step 5
Center and glue a 4- by 3-inch photo on the cover of a composition notebook.

Step 6
Use craft glue to attach 11 tubes vertically on either side of the photo. Glue each tube close to the previous tube so the notebook cover doesn't show through.

Step 7
Glue the remaining 84 tubes on side by side, to cover the front of the notebook. Let dry.

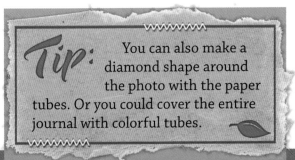

Tip: You can also make a diamond shape around the photo with the paper tubes. Or you could cover the entire journal with colorful tubes.

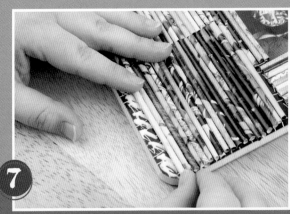

Funny Gifts

The Sunday comics are good for more than just a laugh. They can also make a cute gift bag! Just make sure whoever gets the gift actually opens it. After all, he or she might get stuck reading the comics.

Here's what you need:

- 1 23-inch by 22-inch sheet of newspaper comics, folded to 23 inches by 11 inches
- ruler
- tape
- 2 thin cardboard boxes, such as cereal or cake mix boxes
- scissors
- pencil
- white glue
- hole punch
- 2 pieces of ribbon, 20 inches long

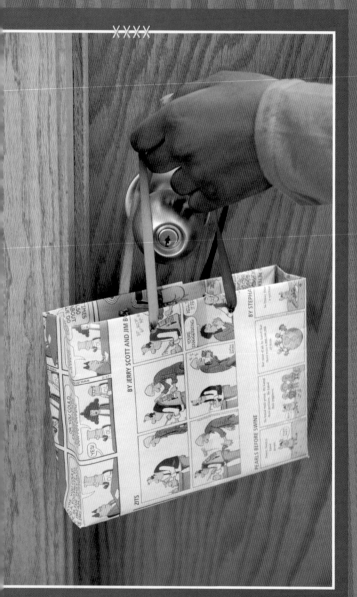

Step 1

Lay the newspaper flat with the folded edge at the top. Fold the top edge over by 1 inch. Tape down the entire folded edge.

Step 2

Wrap the newspaper around one of the boxes so it overlaps by 1 inch at the center of the box. Cut away any paper beyond the 1-inch mark and tape the overlapped edge down. Make sharp folds along the edges of the box.

Step 3

Fold and tape the paper together at the bottom of the box as you would when wrapping a present. (See gift wrapping instructions on page 90.) Do not tape the paper to the box. Make sharp folds along the bottom edges.

Step 4

Slide the box out from the paper and set on the other cardboard box, which has been cut open and laid flat. Trace around one side of the box and cut out. Apply a thin layer of glue to one side of the cardboard and place at the inside bottom of the gift bag.

Step 5

Bring the top edges of the bag together by folding the side edges to the inside. Make sharp folds about halfway down the bag.

Step 6

On one side of the bag, make two holes ½ inch from the top edge and 3 inches apart. Thread ribbon through the holes from outside to inside and tie knots to secure. Repeat on other side of bag.

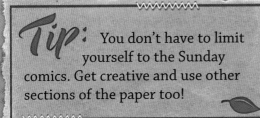

Tip: You don't have to limit yourself to the Sunday comics. Get creative and use other sections of the paper too!

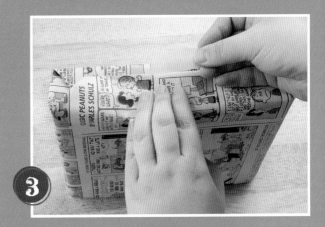

Future Dreamin'

Do you dream of visiting Paris? Dating that guy down the block? Getting a cute, cuddly pup? Capture your goals and dreams in one beautiful collage with this easy vision board. Include places to go, people to meet, goals to achieve—the sky's the limit! Vision boards are popular with the A-list crowd, with fans ranging from President Obama to Oprah. These people believe that creating a picture of what you want makes things more likely to happen. So think big and go forth with glue stick in hand!

Here's what you need:
- magazines
- scissors
- poster board, any size
- glue stick
- markers (optional)
- stickers (optional)

Step 1
Flip through old magazines to find pictures and words that represent things you'd like in your life.

Step 2
Cut out images and words to include on your vision board.

Step 3
Arrange the images any way you like on a piece of poster board.

Step 4
Glue the images to the poster board one at a time.

Step 5 *(not pictured)*
If you want, use markers to write things that are important to you, such as "family." Or add stickers for a finishing touch.

Tip: You can also make a gratitude board to show the things for which you're grateful. It's a fun way to give thanks, which will help you attract more good stuff into your life!

It's a Wrap

Wrapping paper and shopping bags generate 4 million tons (3.6 million metric tons) of trash every year in the United States alone. Yet there's still reason to celebrate. You can do your part to save the planet by creating your own rockin' wrapping paper! Friends and family will love the stylish look of this eco-friendly gift that keeps on giving.

Here's what you need:
- **small gift box**
- **newspaper**
- **scissors**
- **magazines**
- **glue stick**

How to Wrap a Gift

Place the gift face down on the paper. Wrap the paper around the gift and tape the ends of the paper together at the center.

Turn the box so one unwrapped side is facing you. Fold the left and right side flaps in toward the center. Press and smooth the paper down flat over the edges of the gift. Fold the bottom flap up to the center. Fold the top flap to the center and tape down. Repeat on the other unwrapped side of the gift.

1

Step 1

To figure out how much wrapping paper you'll need, place a small gift box on a sheet of newspaper. Cut a square big enough to cover the box by folding ends up and over the top. The paper should overlap by about an inch.

Step 2

Look through magazines for colorful pictures or ads. Cut out an image you like.

Step 3

Use a glue stick to attach the image face up on the newspaper.

Step 4

Continue cutting out images and gluing them to the newspaper. The pictures should overlap each other by about ½ inch. Cover the entire newspaper.

Step 5

Allow all the glue to dry before wrapping the gift.

Tip: Choose a theme that goes with the gift you're giving. Photos of interesting places are great for a travel bag. Pictures of popular musicians would go well with a CD.

Off the Cuff

Wrap your wrist in this eco-friendly beaded cuff! With beads made out of used wrapping paper, this accessory is a gift that keeps on giving. Soon you'll see that going green has never been so stylish.

Here's what you need:
- ruler
- scissors
- used wrapping paper
- glue stick
- round toothpicks
- craft foam
- clear nail polish
- elastic string, about 9 feet long

Step 1
Measure and cut a 10-inch long by 2-inch wide triangle from wrapping paper.

Step 2
Rub a glue stick down the white side of the triangle.

Step 3
Center the toothpick on the wide end of the triangle.

Step 4
Wind the rest of the triangle tightly around the toothpick with the printed side facing outward. Glue the end down.

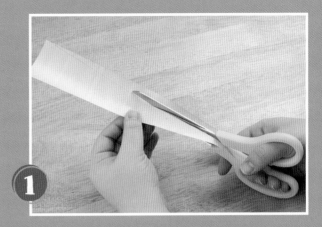

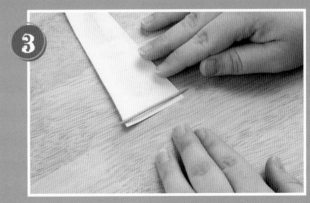

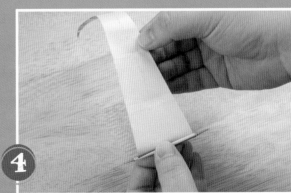

To finish this project, turn to the next page. ⇨

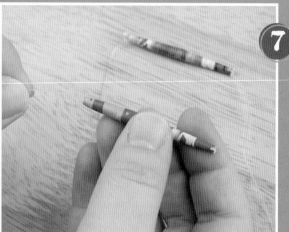

Step 5
Stick the end of the toothpick into a piece of craft foam. Apply two coats of clear nail polish to the paper bead. Avoid getting nail polish on the toothpick. Let dry.

Step 6 *(not pictured)*
Repeat steps 1 through 5 until you have 25 to 30 beads. Remove the toothpicks from inside the paper beads.

Step 7
Thread a piece of elastic string through one bead. Center the bead in the middle of the string. Thread the left end of the string through a second bead.

Step 8
Position the bead so that it lays close to the first bead. You should have both ends of the string on the right side.

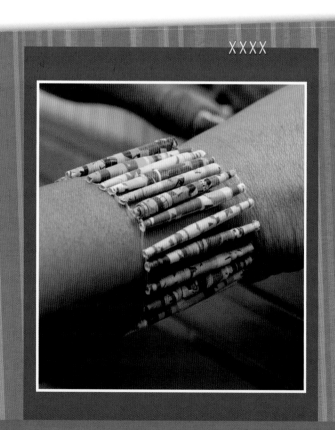

Step 9

Thread the end of the string from the first bead through the second bead. You will have one end of the string on either side of the second bead.

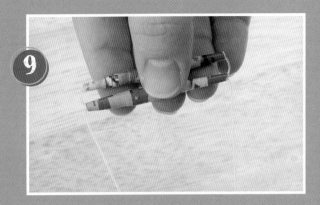

Step 10

Continue adding beads one at a time as in steps 7 through 9. Pull the ends tight to keep the beads laying together flat.

Step 11

When the bracelet is long enough to wrap around your wrist, thread one end of the string through the first bead. Tie both ends together tightly in a knot. Snip off any extra string.

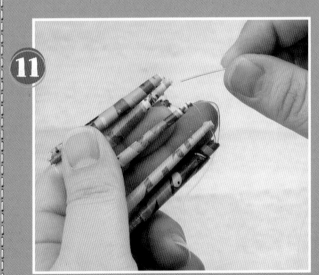

Tip: Spice up the look by adding round beads. Thread beads on the string before and after placing each paper bead.

Pinned Up

From to-do lists to photos, your desk can get messy fast. Give your work space a marvelous makeover with a one-of-a-kind organizer. This do-it-yourself bulletin board keeps all your VIP stuff in one place. Who knew staying tidy could be so cool?

Here's what you need:
- scissors
- ruler
- old T-shirt
- 10- by 15-inch piece of thick cardboard
- glue gun and hot glue
- ribbon, ½-inch wide, 6 feet long
- thumbtacks

1

Step 1

Cut an 11- by 16-inch rectangle from the front or back of an old T-shirt.

Step 2

Center the fabric on the cardboard and wrap it tightly around to the back. Hot glue the fabric edges to the backside of the cardboard.

Step 3

Cut ribbon into four 9-inch strips and two 18-inch strips. Arrange strips in a crisscross pattern on the front of the bulletin board. Use thumbtacks to hold the ribbons in place where they cross.

Step 4

Turn the board over. Pull the end of one ribbon tight to the back of the board and hot glue in place. Repeat with both ends of all ribbons.

Step 5

Use thumbtacks to attach to-do lists and other items to the board. Tuck photos behind ribbons.

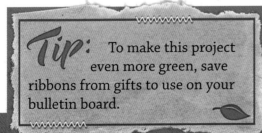

Tip: To make this project even more green, save ribbons from gifts to use on your bulletin board.

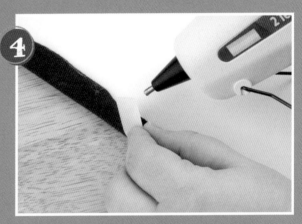

Best Bow

Gift bags and bows can be almost as expensive as the gifts themselves. Do something good for the planet and your budget by creating your own gift wrap accessories. You can start with this neat little bow.

Here's what you need:
- scissors
- ruler
- thin cardboard, such as a cereal box
- 20 strips of used wrapping paper, 4 inches by 1 inch
- clear tape

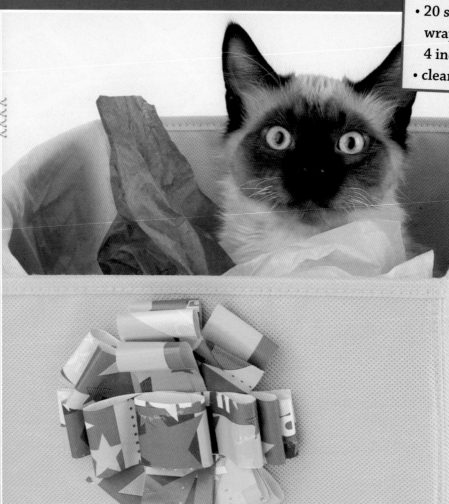

Step 1 *(not pictured)*
Cut a 2-inch square of thin cardboard.

Step 2
Form a loop from one wrapping paper strip with the printed side facing outward. Use a small piece of clear tape to connect the ends of the loop.

Step 3
Use tape to attach the loop to one edge of the cardboard.

Step 4 *(not pictured)*
Continue making and adding loops around the cardboard square.

Step 5
Add more layers of loops to fill out the bow. Place the new loops between previous loops by taping them nearer to the center of the cardboard.

Step 6
Wrap a strip of wrapping paper around two fingers and cut to size. Tape this final loop in the center of the bow.

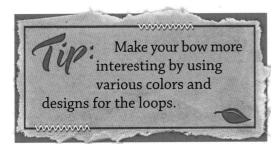
Tip: Make your bow more interesting by using various colors and designs for the loops.

Pressed Paper

Odds are that hardly a day goes by that you don't use paper in dozens of ways. And while most paper is made by machines, making paper at home is easy and fun. Try your hand at recycling wrapping paper into paper pulp. Then form the pulp into a thick piece of paper to spruce up notes, cards, and more. The results are bound to be eco-tastic!

Here's what you need:

- 10 sheets of newspaper
- 4 old towels, each about 12 inches by 8 inches
- used wrapping paper, torn into small pieces to yield 1 cup
- 4 cups hot water
- blender
- 9- by 13-inch pan
- 1 tablespoon white glue
- plastic spoon
- 12- by 8-inch piece of stiff screen
- rolling pin

100

Step 1

Prepare your workspace by placing five sheets of newspaper in a stack. Lay two old towels on top of the newspaper. Set two more towels and five more sheets of newspaper nearby.

Step 2

Combine wrapping paper and hot water in a blender and put on the lid. Let the paper soak for five minutes.

Step 3

Have an adult help you blend the mixture in short bursts on medium-high for 30 to 60 seconds.

Step 4

Pour the pulp into a 9- by 13-inch pan. Add white glue and stir with a plastic spoon.

To finish this project, turn to the next page. ⇨

Step 5
Slide a screen into the bottom of the pan. Move the screen around to cover it evenly with pulp.

Step 6
Carefully remove the screen from the pan, holding it level as you lift it. Hold it over the pan to drain for 1 minute.

Step 7
Set the screen on the newspapers and towels you prepared in step 1. Make sure the pulp is on the top of the screen.

Step 8
Lay the remaining two towels over the screen and pulp. Lay the remaining sheets of newspaper over the towels.

Step 9

Roll a rolling pin over the top newspaper. Repeat several times to squeeze out as much water as you can.

Step 10

Remove the newspapers and towels from the top of the screen. Allow paper to dry on the screen for 24 hours.

Step 11 *(not pictured)*

Place any remaining pulp in the trash. Do not pour pulp down the drain because it can clog pipes.

Step 12

When the paper is completely dry, peel it away from the screen.

Tip: Add glitter or colored thread to the pulp for a more artistic look. Stir these items in after mixing the pulp in the blender.

Stamp of Approval

Plain white envelopes are so yesterday. Nothing says, "Signed, sealed, delivered" like these charming origami-style envelopes! You'll find endless uses for these sassy sleeves. Use them for mailing notes, storing CDs, or sending homemade valentines.

Here's what you need:
- 12- by 12-inch piece of thick used wrapping paper
- craft glue
- sticker

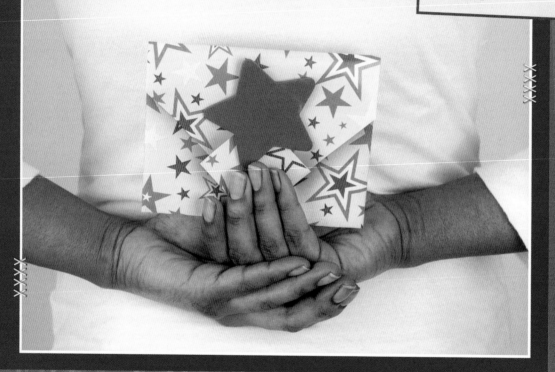

Step 1

Fold a square of wrapping paper in half diagonally to make a triangle. Then fold the top layer of the triangle down to meet the bottom center.

Step 2

Fold the right corner about ⅔ across the triangle. Glue down the bottom edge of this new triangle.

Step 3

Fold the left corner so the point meets the new right corner. Do not glue this triangle yet.

Step 4

Fold the new right corner flap back to the left corner. Glue down the bottom edge of the rest of the triangle made in step 3.

Step 5

Lift the little triangle you made in step 4 so it points straight up. Pull the sides of the triangle outward and flatten into a diamond shape.

Step 6

Once the glue is dry, fold the top of the envelope down to the bottom edge. Close the envelope by tucking the top flap into the diamond-shaped pocket. Secure with a sticker.

Tip: Be sure to use a white address label if sending regular mail. Also keep in mind that square envelopes may require extra postage.

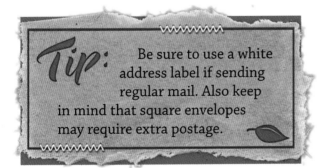

Wrap It Up

You don't need a magic wand to turn everyday items into super-cute containers. All you need is wrapping paper and a little imagination. Turn household items into cases for jewelry, photos, and more with the art of decoupage. With this project, even a used shoebox can become the sassiest storage around.

Here's what you need:
- scissors
- used wrapping paper
- cardboard box with lid
- old newspapers
- sponge brush
- decoupage glue

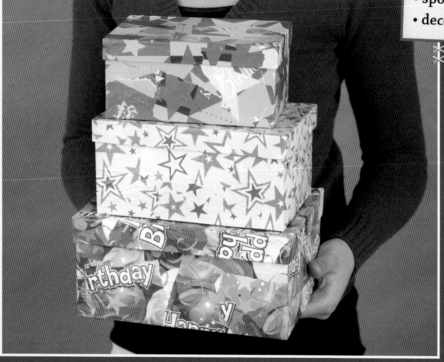

Step 1
Tear or cut used wrapping paper into small pieces. Place a cardboard box and lid on newspaper.

Step 2
Dip a sponge brush in decoupage glue. Apply a thin layer of glue to the back of one wrapping paper piece.

Step 3
Lay the piece flat on the box. Smooth out any wrinkles with your fingers.

Step 4
Cover the piece of wrapping paper and surrounding area with another thin layer of decoupage glue.

Step 5
Repeat steps 2 through 4 until the box and lid are covered with wrapping paper. Let dry for five minutes.

Step 6
Apply a thin layer of decoupage glue over the entire box and lid. Let dry completely before placing the lid on the box.

Tip: You can also use coffee cans and cookie tins for this project.

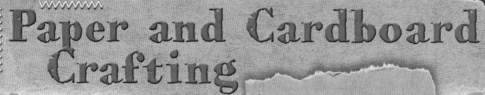

Paper and Cardboard Crafting Facts

🐞 When writing in your notebook or printing papers, be sure to use both sides of the sheet. And don't leave a paper trail. Remember to recycle any old papers or research materials.

🐞 If your school doesn't have a recycling program, consider starting one. You can help reduce the 38 tons (34.5 metric tons) of paper thrown away by schools every year.

🐞 Everyone loves greeting cards, but all that paper can add up. Save some trees by sending cards made of recycled content. Or even better, reuse materials to make your own!

🐞 Next time you get a cardboard package in the mail, don't toss it away! Save the box for future mailings or take it to a nearby recycling center.

Instead of always buying books and magazines, you can borrow some of them from the library. Many libraries have a loan system to help you find books not available at your local library. You'll be lending a green hand by saving a few trees—and some hard-earned cash!

Recycled newspapers become tissue, packaging, and more. In 1989 just 35 percent of newspapers were recycled. Today that number has jumped to more than 73 percent. To help bring that number to 100 percent, make sure your family recycles the newspaper. Read all about it, and then recycle it!

Index

Capstone Press,
1710 Roe Crest Drive
North Mankato, Minnesota 56003.
www.capstonepub.com

Editorial Credits

Lori Shores and Kathryn Clay, editors; Gene Bentdahl, Juliette Peters, and Heidi Thompson,
designers; Sarah Schuette, photo stylist; Marcy Morin, project production; Laura Manthe,
production specialist

Photo Credits

All photos by Capstone Studio/Karon Dubke except Shutterstock/Amy Johansson
(chain link fence) and Ian O'Hanlon (recycling stamp)

Capstone Press thanks ArtStart in St. Paul, Minnesota,
for its contributions to the projects included in this book.

Library of Congress Cataloging-in-Publication Data

Sirrine, Carol.
  Teen crafts : cool projects that look great and help save the planet /
by Carol Sirrine and Jen Jones.
    p. cm.—(Green crafts)
  Includes index.
  ISBN 978-1-4296-6637-4 (paperback)
  1. Handicraft—Juvenile literature. 2. Salvage (Waste, etc.)—Juvenile literature.
  3. Recycling (Waste, etc.)—Juvenile literature. I. Jones, Jen. II. Title.
  TT157.S5288 2011
  745.5—dc22   2011003320

Printed in China.
072012   006837R

About the Authors

A Midwesterner-turned-California girl, Jen Jones loves to be in nature and is proud to be part of any project that makes our world a greener place! Jen is a Los Angeles-based writer who has authored more than 35 books for Capstone Press. Her stories have been published in magazines such as *American Cheerleader, Dance Spirit, Ohio Today,* and *Pilates Style.* She has also written for E! Online, MSN, and PBS Kids, as well as being a web site producer for major talk shows. Jen is a member of the Society of Children's Book Writers and Illustrators.

Carol Sirrine is a former elementary classroom, music, and art teacher. In 1988 she founded ArtStart, an organization that combines learning in the arts with environmental stewardship. ArtStart's ArtScraps, located in St. Paul, Minnesota, combines waste management with art making. In a unique partnership with businesses and manufacturers, ArtScraps collects scraps, overstock, factory rejects, and other items normally destined for the landfill. These products are made available to teachers, parents, artists, Scout leaders, and day-care providers.